The Creative Cast Iron Cookbook: 50 Clever, Delectable, and Easy to Make Cast Iron Dinner Recipes

Disclaimer and Terms of Use: Effort has been made to ensure that the information in this book is accurate and complete, however, the author and the publisher do not warrant the accuracy of the information, text and graphics contained within the book due to the rapidly changing nature of science, research, known and unknown facts and Internet. The Author and the publisher do not hold any responsibility for errors, omissions or contrary interpretation of the subject matter herein. This book is presented solely for motivational and informational purposes only.

Table of Contents

Chicken Tortilla Skillet Dinner 45

Easy Chicken Dinner 47

Festive Garlic Shrimp 49

Curried Salmon and Eggplant 50

Country Skillet Dinner 51

Philly Style Steak Pizza 52

Broccoli Rabe and Bean Skillet 54

Couscous Chicken 56

Italian Halibut and Sage Skillet 57

Roasted Chicken and Vegetables 58

Stuffed and Baked Skillet Rigatoni 60

Tamale Pie with Green Chilies 62

Chicken Sauerkraut Skillet 64

Chicken Pot Pie 65

Seafood Paella 67

Walnut and Maple Chicken 69

Sweet Red Peppers and Lamb 71

Pear Curry 73

Chicken Tacos 74

Beef Teriyaki Stir Fry 75

Broiled Shrimps with White Beans 77

Barley Mushroom Pilaf 78

Pan Grilled Steak Chermoula 80

Spiced Sirloin Steak 81

Trout with Lemon and Herb 82

Gnocchi Chicken Sausage Skillet 83

Book Description

Cooking dinners for your family is something almost everyone takes pride in. It is indeed one of the most important meals of the day and what better way to show your love and affection for your family then by cooking healthy meals.

This book is intended to re-introduce you to the concept of cast-iron cooking and show just how healthy it can be for both you and your family. So whether you are following a paleo diet or are a hard core vegan or even if you like your meals gluten free, you can now easily adapt towards a cast-iron lifestyle by making just a few simple changes in your cooking.

Out of all the cookware that are present in the marketplace, cast-iron cooking has been gaining increasing popularity. These are the most multipurpose cooking utensils one can possibly have in their kitchen. Not only are the cast-iron skillets and ovens outstanding heat conductors, but they also possess the flexibility that makes your food preparation much easier. Cast-iron cookware can cook exceptionally at any heat, in the oven or on the stovetop, with almost any type of food.

A Little bit of History

Cast-iron is essentially iron that is emptied into a mold to produce useful devices. The pans and pots of cast-iron are made in this manner. Pots as well as cauldrons were formerly made from brass since iron could not be functioned until heaters creating sufficient amount of heat to melt it were designed (around 513 B.C. in China and England). Currently, pots could be prepared by constructing molds from sand and pouring molting metal in the mold. The unique cooking pots normally had three legs since they were planned to be utilized over an open fire. Cook tops with tops for food preparation did not come in the usual use until 1700s. This permitted tremendous progression in cookware, particularly cast-iron food preparation when pots and pans activated to be made in bulk quantities.

Cast-iron skillet vs. Cast-iron Dutch Oven

Cast-iron cookware comes in a diversity of sizes and shapes. They are famous in the form of a frying pan or else a skillet. This is the weighty pan you see being flourished as a weapon by womenfolk in some of the typical westerns. However, its rugged building and smooth interior surface make it high quality. It frequently comes in ten to twelve inch sizes. A cast-iron skillet can be utilized for frying eggs, Reuben sandwiches, pancakes, hamburgers, chicken, and much more.

Dutch ovens, on the other hand, are usually utilized for baking and are, at times, covered. A Dutch oven consists of a lid to hold in the dampness. It can be utilized for a wide diversity of dishes counting the now well-known, six-hour stew. An oven with limbs is often named as a camp Dutch oven since it can be utilized over an exposed fire.

Caring for Cast-iron

Certainly, some maintenance goes into upholding cast-iron cookware. New cast-iron cookware's frequently come with a waxy covering or else shellac, which must be detached with hot foam-covered water prior to seasoning. When cleaning a piece of cast-iron cookware, simply make use of slightly foamy water. A rough pad is satisfactory to eliminate coated on food particles, nonetheless, it is finest not to smear the scrubbing device too strongly. Cast-iron must never be washed in the dishwasher. By no means, dip a hot pot in icy water as it might crack.

Cast-iron Cooking like a Pro

When a pleasure-loving chef steps into the kitchenette to make a masterpiece, numerous elements comes in to pay to his eventual masterpiece. One of those fundamentals is the utensils he uses and exactly the cookware used to make his dishes. There are an amount of different fragments of cast-iron cookware, each attending a special aim, and making food preparation a special involvement. Having and making use of cast-iron cookware will profit your family for ages to come.

Any individual who has ever had the benefit of cooking with a very much prepared cast-iron skillet might think about cast-iron cookware's adaptable cooking capacities. What numerous individuals do not understand is that there are various points of interest that cast-iron cookware has over other cookware materials.

1. You can Prepare with less oil when you make use of a Cast-Iron Pan

   That dazzling shine on cast-iron cookware is the indication of an all-around prepared dish, which renders it essentially non-stick. The well-being reward, obviously, is that you will not have to utilize copious amounts of oil to coat fresh potatoes or burn chicken when cooking in cast-iron. To flavor your cast-iron skillet, shelter the base of the dish with a thick coat of proper salt and cooking oil, then warm until the oil begins to smoke. Painstakingly empty the salt as well as oil into a dish, and then utilize a portion of paper towels to rub within the container until it is smooth. To wash cast-iron, never utilize cleanser. Essentially, scrub the skillet with a hardened brush and boiling water and dry it totally.

2. Cast-iron is a Chemical-free Substitute to Non-stick Pots

   Another advantage of utilizing a cast-iron dish instead of a non-stick container is that you can maintain a strategic distance from the destructive chemicals that are found in a non-stick skillet. The anti-agents covering that keeps foods from adhering to non-stick pots and skillets contains PFCs (perfluorocarbons), a compound that is connected to liver harm, distortion, formative issues, and as indicated by one 2011 reading in the Paper of Clinical Endocrinology & Metabolism, premature menopause. PFCs are discharged and breathed in from non-stick contains as exhaust when dishes are warmed on high warmth. In like manner, we can consume them when the surface of the dish is scratched. Both standard and fire covered cast-iron containers are awesome substitutes for a non-stick skillet for this cause.

3. Food Preparation with cast-iron Strengthens your Diet with Iron

   Though cast-iron does not filter substances, it can drain some iron in your food and that is something to be thankful for. Iron deficiency is very common all across the globe, particularly amongst ladies. Truth be told, 10% of American people are iron-deficient. Preparing food; particularly something acidic such as tomato sauce in a cast-iron pan can build iron substance, by as much as twenty times.

4. Even Heating Area
   Different from stainless steel as well as aluminum, cast-iron cookware provides an even warming area for food preparation no matter what kind of cooking exterior you use. This is very advantageous when making food over an open fire.

5. Naturally Non-Stick

   A very prepared cast-iron skillet or else cast-iron oven gets to be characteristically non-stick when prepared correctly. This regular non-stick trademark offers another focal point over stainless steel as well as aluminum cookware too. Different from other materials, seasoned cast-iron removes the want for using oil or else butter on the cooking exterior, making your diet lower in fat.

6. Ease

One of the most important benefits of cast-iron cookware is its cost effectiveness as compared to that of like quality aluminum or else stainless-steel cookware. You can generally find a superiority cast-iron saucepan or else cast-iron griddle for a portion of the cost you would disburse for other materials.

50 Delicious Cast-iron Dinner Recipes for Your Family

Ingredients:

- 14 oz. smoked sausage, sliced
- 1 tbsp. olive oil
- 1 bell pepper, diced
- ½ red bell pepper, diced
- 1 onion, diced
- 2 tbsp. olive oil
- 2 potatoes, diced
- 1 tsp. salt
- 1 tsp. black pepper

Directions:

1. Heat 2 tbsp. of oil in a large cast-iron skillet over medium-high heat. Add diced potatoes and stir in salt and ground black pepper. Cook about 8 to 10 minutes or until potatoes are golden brown and fork tender. Stir frequently during cooking to avoid burning. Remove from heat.

2. In separate skillet, add 1 tbsp. oil and cook smoked sausage over medium-high heat for 5 minutes or until sausage is brown. Remove sausage from pan and set aside.

3. Add peppers and onions to skillet, stirring constantly, cook for 5 minutes or until peppers are tender. Remove from heat.

4. Add sausage, peppers, and onions to the cast-iron skillet with the potatoes. Mix together over medium heat until well combined and all ingredients are heated through.

Nutritional Information:

Calories: 526, Fats: 38.9 grams,
Carbohydrates: 22.3 grams, Protein: 21.9
grams

Serves: 4
Cooking Time: 35 minutes

Ingredients:

- 1 pound beef tenderloin (cut into 4 steaks)
- 1 tsp. onion (minced dried)
- 1 tsp. salt
- 1 tsp. freshly ground pepper
- 2 tbsp. vegetable oil
- 2 large onions, thinly sliced
- 1/3 cup dry sherry
- 1 tbsp. all-purpose flour
- 1 cup beef broth
- 2 tsp. thyme, chopped
- 4 slices whole-grain baguette (½ inch thick), toasted
- ½ cup Swiss cheese, shredded

Directions:

1. Over medium-high, heat 1 tbsp. of vegetable oil in large cast-iron skillet.

2. Mix together dried onions, salt, and ground black pepper and sprinkle over steaks. Reduce heat to medium and add steaks to skillet. Cook each side about 3 to 6 minutes for medium-rare, 3 to 4 minutes longer on each side for well done. Remove steaks to a plate, cover, and set aside.

3. Place oven rack in the upper third of oven and preheat broiler.

4. To skillet, add remaining oil, onions, and dry sherry. Turn heat to medium-high; cover and cook for 10 to 12 minutes or until onions are golden brown and tender and liquid has evaporated. Stir frequently to avoid burning.

5. Sprinkle flour over onions and mix until well coated. Stir in beef broth and add thyme and remaining ½

tsp of salt. Cook, stirring constantly, until gravy is thick and bubbly, about 1 minute.

6. Remove skillet from heat and add steaks and any meat juices to the skillet. Spoon the onion gravy over steaks, top each steak with a baguette slice, and sprinkle with cheese.

7. Carefully place skillet in oven and broil about 2 minutes or until cheese is brown and bubbly.

8. Serve on individual plates topped with onion gravy.

Nutritional Information:
Calories: 377, Fats: 18 grams, Carbohydrates: 20 grams, Protein: 31 grams

Serves: 4
Cooking Time: 45 minutes

Ingredients:

- 6 oz. wild rice
- 5 chicken breasts (boneless, skinless)
- 3 tbsp. all-purpose flour
- 2 tsp. rosemary, dried and crushed
- 1/8 tsp. black pepper
- 2 tbsp. olive oil
- 1 cup baby carrots
- 1 cup chopped onion
- 2 tsp. garlic, minced
- 1 cup water
- 1 can chicken broth
- 2 cups spinach (chopped)

Directions:

1. Heat 1 tbsp. olive oil in large cast-iron skillet over medium heat.

2. Sprinkle chicken with 1 ½ tbsp. of seasoning mix from the wild and white rice seasoning packet. Set remaining seasoning mix aside.

3. In shallow dish, combine flour, rosemary, and black pepper and dredge chicken breasts through flour mixture.

4. Add chicken to hot skillet and cook each side for 3 to 4 minutes or until brown. Remove chicken to a paper towel lined plate and set aside.

5. Add remaining olive oil to skillet and heat over medium. Add carrots, onions and garlic and sauté for 2 minutes.

6. To vegetable mixture, add water and chicken broth. Increase heat to high and bring to a boil. Stir in remainder of seasoning packet and wild rice, mix well.

7. Add chicken breasts to skillet, cover and reduce heat to low. Simmer for 15 minutes or chicken is cooked through.

Nutritional Information:
Calories: 480, Fats: 10 grams, Carbohydrates: 57.9 grams, Protein: 36 grams

Serves: 4
Cooking Time: 30 minutes

Ingredients:
- 1 tbsp. vegetable oil
- 4 turkey breasts (boneless)
- 1 tsp. salt
- 1 tsp. ground black pepper
- 1 ½ cups milk
- 1 can condensed cream of chicken soup
- 2 cups rice, uncooked
- 2 cups asparagus
- 1 cup cheddar cheese (shredded)
- ¼ cup sliced almonds

Directions:

1. Heat oil in large cast-iron skillet over medium-high heat. Season the turkey with salt and pepper and add to skillet. Cook each side for 3 to 4 minutes or until meat is cooked through and lightly browned. Remove the turkey to a plate and cover.

2. Add soup and milk to skillet, mix well, raise heat and bring to a boil. Stir in rice and asparagus and lay the turkey on top. Sprinkle cheese and almonds over top. Reduce heat to low, cover and cook for 5 minutes.

3. Serve over bed of rice or buttered noodles.

Nutritional Information:
Calories: 426, Fats: 13.1 grams, Carbohydrates: 58.3 grams, Protein: 18.2 grams

Serves: 6
Cooking Time: 35 minutes

Smothered Mushroom Chicken

Ingredients:
- ¾ cup all-purpose flour
- ¼ tsp. salt
- 1/8 tsp. ground black pepper
- 4 chicken leg (quartered)
- 2 tbsp. vegetable oil
- 3 tbsp. butter
- 1 small onion, chopped
- 8 oz. fresh white mushrooms, sliced
- 1 cup chicken broth
- ½ cup dry white wine

Directions:

1. Heat oil in a large cast-iron skillet over medium-high heat.

2. Combine flour, salt, and ground black pepper in a shallow dish. Dredge chicken through flour, coating well. Add chicken to hot oil and cook each side, 4 to 5 minutes or until golden brown. Remove chicken to a paper towel lined plate, cover and set aside.

3. Melt butter in skillet and add onions and sliced mushrooms. Sauté for 5 to 7 minutes, stirring frequently to keep from burning.

4. Mix in chicken broth and white wine. Bring to a hard boil, then reduce heat to low. Add chicken to mushroom gravy, cover and let simmer for 10 to 15 minutes, or until chicken is cooked through and juices run clear. Turn chicken once during cooking.

5. Serve chicken and mushroom gravy over a bed of rice or noodles.

Nutritional Information:
Calories: 480, Fats: 9 grams, Carbohydrates: 40.4 grams, Protein: 36 grams

Serves: 4
Cooking Time: 35 minutes

Ingredients:

- 16 ounces linguine
- 1 can crushed tomatoes
- 8 oz. vegetable stock
- 2 ½ cups water
- 1/3 cup Greek yogurt
- 2 tbsp. hot sauce
- 1 red onion, sliced
- 8 cloves garlic, sliced
- 1 red bell pepper, sliced
- 1 green bell pepper, sliced
- ½ tsp. red pepper flakes
- 1 tbsp. salt
- 1 tsp. cumin
- ¾ tsp. chili powder
- ¼ tsp. ground oregano
- 2 sprigs cilantro
- 3 tbsp. extra-virgin olive oil
- 1 tsp. ground black pepper
- limes, for serving

Directions:

1. In a 12 inch cast-iron skillet, combine linguini, tomatoes, stock, hot sauce, onion, garlic, red and green peppers, red pepper flakes, cilantro, oil, salt, cumin, chili powder, oregano, pepper, and water. Mix well and bring to boil over high heat.

2. Continue to boil on high, stirring and turning pasta frequently. Boil about 11 minutes or until pasta is cooked and the sauce has nearly evaporated. Remove from heat.

3. Remove any visible cilantro stems and stir in Greek yogurt until well blended.

4. Garnish with cilantro and serve while hot.

Nutritional Information:
Calories: 347, Fats: 9.9 grams, Carbohydrates: 52.2 grams, Protein: 13.7 grams

Serves: 4 to 6
Cooking Time: 25 minutes

Ingredients:
- 2 heads garlic, cloves separated
- 8 chicken drumsticks
- 3 tbsp. extra virgin olive oil
- 1/3 cup white wine
- 1 cup chicken broth
- 2 tsp. dijon mustard
- 2 tsp. all-purpose flour
- 1/3 cup chives chopped
- 1 tsp. salt
- 1 tsp. freshly ground pepper

Directions:

1. With side of large chef knife, smash garlic cloves to loosen skins. Peel cloves and cut in half, set aside.

2. Sprinkle chicken with ½ tsp. salt and ½ tsp. ground black pepper.

3. Heat oil in large cast-iron skillet over medium heat. Add garlic and cook about 2 minutes or until just turning brown. With slotted spoon, remove garlic to plate.

4. Add chicken to skillet and cook for 4 minutes until brown. Turn chicken over and add garlic and wine to skillet, cook for 1 minute.

5. In small bowl, add chicken broth, mustard, ¼ tsp. salt, and flour, whisking until smooth. Add broth mixture to skillet and bring to boil. Reduce to medium-low, bringing to a simmer. Cover skillet and cook chicken for 8 to 10 minutes and chicken is cooked through.

6. Sprinkle chives or scallion greens over top and serve while hot.

Nutritional Information:
Calories: 343 Fats: 17grams, Carbohydrates: 7 grams,
Protein: 35 grams

Serves: 4
Cooking Time: 40 minutes

Ingredients:
- 1 tbsp. butter
- 1 can sauerkraut, un-drained
- 2/3 cup uncooked rice
- 1 medium onion, chopped
- 1 pound ground beef, browned
- 1 ¼ tsp. salt
- 1 ¼ tsp. pepper
- 1 can tomato sauce
- 1 tsp. sugar

Directions:

1. Melt butter in 10-inch cast-iron skillet. Layer sauerkraut over butter.

2. Sprinkle rice over top of sauerkraut.

3. In this order, one at a time, layer the following ingredients over the rice: ground beef, salt, pepper, tomato sauce, and sugar.

4. Cover and cook over low heat until rice is fluffy.

Nutritional Information:
Calories: 261, Fats: 6.9 grams, Carbohydrates: 23 grams, Protein: 25.6 grams

Serves: 4 to 6
Cooking Time: 35 minutes

Ingredients:

- 10 lasagna noodles, broken
- 28 oz. tomato can with juice
- 1 tbsp. oil
- 1 onion, diced
- 3 garlic cloves, minced
- pinch of red pepper flakes
- 1 tsp. dried Italian seasoning
- 1 lb. sausage crumbled
- 1/2 cup mozzarella cheese (shredded)
- ½ cup Parmesan cheese (grated)
- ½ cup ricotta cheese
- 1 tsp. salt
- 1 tsp. ground black pepper
- 3 tbsp. fresh basil (optional)

Directions:

1. Coarsely chop the tomatoes and set aside.

2. Heat oil over medium heat in a large cast-iron skillet. Add onion and cook 5-7 minutes, until onions are tender and translucent. Add salt, pepper, garlic, red pepper flakes, and Italian seasoning. Mix well and cook about 30 seconds or just until fragrant.

3. Mix in crumbled sausage. Stirring frequently, cook until meat is no long pink. Spread broken lasagna noodles over sausage and top with tomatoes and the juice. Increase heat to medium-high and allow it to simmer. Cover and cook, stirring frequently, about 20-24 minutes or until pasta is tender.

4. Place oven rack in the upper third of oven and preheat broiler. When pasta is cooked, remove from heat and stir in ¼ cup of ricotta cheese and half the mozzarella and parmesan cheeses. Evenly dot

remaining ricotta cheese over the top of pasta. Layer with remaining mozzarella and parmesan and carefully place skillet under oven broiler.

5. Broil about 5 minutes, until cheese is brown and bubbly.

6. Remove from oven and sprinkle with fresh basil if desired.

Nutritional Information:
Calories: 795, Fats: 27.7 grams, Carbohydrates: 47.4 grams, Protein: 33.6 grams

Serves: 4
Cooking Time: 35 minutes

Ingredients:
- 1 ½ pounds shrimp, large, unpeeled
- 9 oz. pre-cooked linguine
- ¼ cup butter
- ¼ cup olive oil
- ¼ cup green onions (chopped)
- 2 garlic cloves, minced
- 1 tbsp. dry white wine
- 2 tsp. fresh lemon juice
- ½ tsp. salt
- ½ tsp. ground pepper
- 1 tbsp. dill (chopped)
- 1 tbsp. parsley (chopped)

Directions:

1. Peel and devein shrimp, leaving tails on.

2. Prepare linguine by dropping in hot water (not boiling) for 30 seconds. Drain and set aside.

3. In large cast-iron skillet, melt butter over medium-high heat. Add green onions and garlic and sauté, stirring constantly for 4 to 5 minutes or until onions are translucent.

4. To the butter and onion mixture, add shrimp, wine, lemon juice, salt, and ground black pepper. Reduce heat to medium and cook, stirring constantly, until shrimp turns pink, about 3 to 5 minutes.

5. Add fresh dill and parsley and mix well. With a slotted spoon, remove shrimp, leaving sauce in skillet.

6. Add cooked pasta to skillet, tossing until coated with sauce. Remove from heat and top with shrimp or

transfer linguine to a serving bowl and top with shrimp.

Nutritional Information:
Calories: 728, Fats: 49.9 grams, Carbohydrates: 42.9 grams, Protein: 24.4 grams

Serves: 4
Cooking Time: 20 minutes

Ingredients:

- 8 ounces sirloin steak, cut into thin slices
- 8 ounces brown rice noodles (packaged)
- ½ cup dry sherry
- 4 tsp. black bean garlic sauce
- 1 tbsp. reduced sodium soy sauce
- 2 tsp. brown sugar
- 2 tsp. cornstarch
- 4 tsp. canola oil
- 1 tsp. ginger, minced
- 1 onion, sliced
- 1 bag Asian stir-fry vegetables
- ½ cup water

Directions:

1. Bring large pot of water to boil. Add rice noodles and cook according to package directions. Stir frequently to avoid sticking. Drain noodles and rinse with cold water. Set aside.

2. In a small bowl, combine dry sherry, black bean garlic sauce, soy sauce, brown sugar, and cornstarch and set aside.

3. In large cast-iron skillet, heat 2 tbsp. oil over medium-high heat. Add ginger and reduce heat to medium, cook for 30 seconds, add onion and stir constantly, cook 1 to 3 minutes or until onion is tender.

4. Add Asian stir-fry vegetables and ¼ cup water. Cover and cook vegetables 2-4 minutes until tender, stirring occasionally. Transfer vegetables to bowl with noodles then dry skillet.

5. Add remaining 2 tbsp. oil to skillet and heat over medium-high. Add sliced steak and cook 1 to 3

minutes until brown, while stirring constantly. Add bean sauce mixture to skillet and cook 1 to 2 minutes or until sauce is slightly thickened.

6. Add noodles, vegetables, and ¼ cup water to skillet. Mix well to coat noodles and vegetables and cook another 2 minutes until heated through.

Nutritional Information:
Calories: 381, Fats: 8 grams, Carbohydrates: 17 grams, Protein: 15 grams

Serves: 4
Cooking Time: 30 minutes

Ingredients:
- 1 pound ground beef
- 1 tbsp. vegetable oil
- ½ cup diced onion
- 2 cups hot water
- 1 lb. can tomatoes (diced)
- ¼ cup Heinz 57 sauce
- 2 tsp. salt
- 1 tsp. sugar
- 1 tsp. ground black pepper
- 1 cup elbow macaroni, uncooked

Directions:

1. Heat oil in large cast-iron skillet over medium-high heat. Cook ground beef until brown, add onion and cook until translucent. Drain excess fat.

2. Stir in water, diced tomatoes, Heinz 57 sauce, salt, sugar, and ground black pepper.

3. Turn heat to high and bring mixture to a boil. Stir in macaroni and reduce heat to low. Simmer uncovered for 15 to 20 minutes until macaroni is tender. Stir frequently to keep from sticking.

Nutritional Information:
Calories: 305, Fats: 8.8 grams, Carbohydrates: 23.7 grams, Protein: 31.3 grams

Serves: 5
Cooking Time: 20 minutes

Ingredients:
- 2 tbsp. vegetable oil
- 6 loin chops
- 4 potatoes, sliced
- 6 carrots, quartered
- 1 cup sliced onions
- 2/3 cup green bell peppers; coarsely diced
- 1 tsp. salt
- 1 tsp. ground black pepper
- 1 can tomato soup
- ½ cup water
- ¼ tsp. Tabasco sauce

Directions:

1. Heat oil in large cast-iron skillet over medium-high heat. Add pork chops and brown, about 3 minutes each side. Cover and cook another 15 minutes. Remove pork chops to a plate and drain fat from skillet.

2. Layer vegetables in skillet, in this order, sprinkling each layer with salt and pepper: potatoes, carrots, onions, and green bell peppers. Top vegetables with pork chops.

3. In mixing bowl, combine soup, water, and Tabasco. Whisk together until smooth. Pour over pork chops and vegetables. Raise heat to high and bring to a hard simmer, then reduce heat to medium, cover and simmer for 45 minutes or until pork chops and vegetables are tender.

Nutritional Information:
Calories: 631, Fats: 37.2 grams, Carbohydrates: 45.5 grams, Protein: 27.7 grams

Serves: 4 to 6

Cooking Time: 35 minutes

Ingredients:
- 18 oz. package ziti pasta
- 1 tbsp. olive oil
- 1 pound ground turkey
- 12 oz. jar roasted bell peppers
- ¼ cup sun dried tomato pesto
- 23 ounce jar marinara sauce
- 1 cup parmesan cheese, grated

Directions:

1. Cook ziti pasta al dente, according to package directions. Drain and set aside.

2. Heat 1 tbsp. of oil in a large cast-iron skillet over medium-high heat. Crumble ground turkey into skillet cook 5 to 7 minutes until meat is brown and cooked through. Remove to plate and set aside. Discard any grease left from cooking.

3. Place roasted red peppers and pesto in food processor or blender and pulse until smooth and creamy.

4. Add red pepper puree and marinara sauce to cooked sausage. Turn heat to medium high and stir until meat is distributed throughout the sauce. Turn heat to low, cover and simmer for 30 minutes.

5. Add ziti pasta to sauce and cook until heated through, about 2 to 3 minutes. Stir frequently to keep from sticking.

6. Sprinkle cheese over top of pasta and continue cooking until cheese is melted.

Nutritional Information:
Calories: 704, Fats: 29.9 grams, Carbohydrates: 60 grams, Protein: 45.2 grams

Serves: 4
Cooking Time: 35 minutes

Ingredients:
- 2 slices bacon
- 1 cup onion, chopped
- 1/3 cup green bell pepper, chopped
- 1 pound ground beef
- 1 tbsp. sugar
- 1 tsp. ground black pepper
- 16 ounce canned tomatoes (peeled diced)
- 5 ounces elbow macaroni (uncooked)
- 8 ounces cheddar cheese, shredded

Directions:

1. Cook bacon in cast-iron skillet over medium heat until crispy. Remove to paper towel lined plate. When cool, crumble bacon and return to skillet.

2. Add onion and green bell peppers to skillet and cook until tender. Add ground beef and cook until browned.

3. Add tomatoes, sugar, and black pepper and mix well and bring to boil over medium-high heat. Stir in macaroni, cover and reduce heat to low. Simmer for 20 minutes, stirring occasionally, until macaroni is tender.

4. Sprinkle shredded cheese over top and heat until melted.

Nutritional Information:
Calories: 446, Fats: 20.4 grams, Carbohydrates: 25.6 grams, Protein: 38.8 grams

Serves: 6
Cooking Time: 35 minutes

Ingredients:
- 8 ounces whole wheat penne
- 16 ounce bag pepper and onion mix (frozen)
- 6 ounces turkey sausage, crumbled
- 2 8 ounce cans tomato sauce
- 1 tsp. garlic powder
- 1 tsp. dried oregano
- ¼ tsp. salt
- ½ cup cottage cheese
- ¾ cup Italian cheese, shredded

Directions:

1. Add pasta to a large pot of salted, boiling water and cook according to package directions; al dente. Drain and set aside.

2. While pasta is cooking, heat a large cast-iron skillet over medium-high heat. Add frozen vegetables and sausage to skillet. Stirring frequently, cook about 10 to 15 minutes or until liquid from vegetables has evaporated.

3. Position oven rack in the top third of oven and preheat broiler.

4. Add tomato sauce, garlic powder, oregano, and salt to vegetables and sausage. Mix well and reduce heat to medium-low. Add cottage cheese and pasta and mix well. Cook about 2 minutes, stirring constantly and pasta is heated through.

5. Sprinkle cheese over top of pasta and carefully place skillet under broiler. Broil for 1 to 2 minutes or until cheese is brown.

Nutritional Information:

Calories: 430 Fats: 10 grams, Carbohydrates: 61 grams, Protein: 11 grams

Serves: 4
Cooking Time: 30 minutes

Ingredients:
- 1 pound ground beef
- 1 tbsp. vegetable oil
- ½ cup diced onion
- 1 tsp. chili powder
- 1 (16 ounce) can diced tomatoes
- 1 (16 ounce) can whole kernel corn, drained
- 1 ½ cup beef broth
- ½ cup sliced green bell pepper
- 1 ½ cup Minute Rice

Directions:

1. Heat vegetable oil in large cast-iron skillet over medium-high heat. Add ground beef, onions, and chili powder and cook 5 minutes until beef is browned.

2. Add tomatoes, beef broth, corn, and bell peppers to beef mixture. Bring to boil and add rice.

3. Cook for 10 minutes, stirring frequently, until rice has absorbed moisture.

Nutritional Information:
Calories: 559, Fats: 11.9 grams, Carbohydrates: 67.4 grams, Protein: 42.9 grams

Serves: 4 to 6
Cooking Time: 25 minutes

Ingredients:
- 1 tbsp. vegetable oil
- 4 small chicken breasts (boneless, skinless)
- 1 tsp. salt
- 1 tsp. ground black pepper
- 1 ½ cups milk
- 1 can cream of chicken soup
- 2 cups rice, uncooked
- 2 cups asparagus
- 1 cup shredded cheddar cheese
- ¼ cup sliced almonds

Directions:

1. Heat oil in large cast-iron skillet over medium-high heat. Season chicken with salt and pepper and add to skillet. Cook each side for 3 to 4 minutes or until meat is cooked through and lightly browned. Remove chicken to a plate and cover.

2. Add soup and milk to skillet, mix well, raise heat and bring to a boil. Stir in rice and asparagus and lay chicken on top. Sprinkle cheese and almonds over top. Reduce heat to low, cover and cook for 5 minutes.

3. Serve over bed of rice or buttered noodles.

Nutritional Information:
Calories: 722, Fats: 33.5 grams, Carbohydrates: 68.5 grams, Protein: 43.5 grams

Serves: 4
Cooking Time: 35 minutes

Ingredients:
- 1 tbsp. olive oil
- 1 pound rib eye, thinly sliced
- 1 onion, sliced
- 2 bell peppers, sliced
- 1 cup mushrooms, chopped
- 2 tbsp. soy sauce
- 1 tbsp. Worcestershire sauce
- 1 tbsp. lemon juice
- 1 tbsp. dried basil
- ½ tbsp. minced garlic
- 1 tsp. salt
- 1 tsp. ground black pepper
- 4 slices provolone

Directions:

1. Add olive oil to a large cast-iron skillet. Over medium-high heat, add sliced steak and cook until slightly browned.

2. Add soy sauce, Worcestershire sauce, lemon juice, dried basil, garlic, salt, and ground black pepper. Stir until mixed thoroughly.

3. Add onion, peppers, and mushrooms, mix well and cook about 10 minutes or until vegetables are browned and tender. Stir frequently to avoid burning.

4. Layer cheese slices over meat and let melt. Remove from heat and serve over rice or on hoagie rolls.

Nutritional Information:
Calories: 377, Fats: 18 grams, Carbohydrates: 20 grams, Protein: 31 grams

Serves: 4
Cooking Time: 25 minutes

Ingredients:

- 2 chicken breasts, boneless, skinless
- 2 tbsp. vegetable oil
- 1 shallot, minced
- 2 cloves garlic, minced
- 2 tbsp. chipotle peppers in Adobo sauce, minced
- ½ tsp. salt
- 1 ¾ cups chicken broth
- 5 cups tortilla chips
- 1 large tomato, chopped
- 1 cup cheddar cheese, shredded
- 2 tbsp. cilantro, chopped

Directions:

1. With paper towels, pat chicken dry and sprinkle with salt and pepper.
2. Heat 1 tbsp. of oil in a large cast-iron skillet over medium-high heat. Add chicken and cook 5 to 7 minutes on each side, until golden brown. Remove to plate and set aside.
3. Add remaining oil to skillet and add shallot, garlic, chipotle peppers, and salt. Cook over medium-high heat for 30 seconds until vegetables become fragrant.
4. Deglaze pan by adding chicken broth and scraping browned bits from bottom of skillet, then bring broth to a simmer.
5. Add 2 ½ cups broken tortilla chips to the broth, then layer chicken on top, pushing down into the broth. Reduce heat to medium low and simmer for 10 to 15 minutes and chicken is cooked through. Remove chicken from broth and place on cutting board. Let rest for 5 minutes, then chop into bite-size pieces.

6. Return chicken to skillet and add tomato, ½ cup cheddar cheese, and 1 tbsp. cilantro, mix well. Stir in remaining tortilla chips, just until moistened and incorporated into broth.

7. Move oven rack to upper third of oven and preheat broiler.

8. Spread remaining cheddar cheese over top of chicken mixture and place in oven. Broil for 2 to 3 minutes or until cheese is brown and bubbly. Remove from oven and top with remaining cilantro.

9. Let casserole sit for 5 minutes before serving.

Nutritional Information:
Calories: 416, Fats: 23.2 grams, Carbohydrates: 19.6 grams, Protein: 32 grams

Serves: 4
Cooking Time: 25 minutes

Ingredients:
- ½ cup flour
- 1 tbsp. paprika
- ½ tsp. salt
- 1 chicken, cut into pieces, skinned
- ¼ cup butter
- 4 medium potatoes, peeled and quartered
- 4 carrots, halved and cut in strips
- 1 can cream of chicken soup
- 1 cup sour cream

Directions:

1. In large cast-iron skillet, melt butter over medium heat.

2. In shallow bowl, combine flour, paprika, and salt. Dredge chicken pieces in flour mixture and cook 5 minutes on each side until lightly browned. Add potatoes and carrots and distribute with chicken pieces.

3. In mixing bowl, combine soup and 1 can full of water. Whisk together until smooth. Pour over chicken and vegetables. Raise heat to high and bring to a hard simmer. Reduce heat to low and simmer for 40 minutes or until chicken and vegetables are tender.

4. Remove chicken and vegetables to a serving platter.

5. Whisk sour cream into drippings and heat to serving temperature. Serve with chicken and vegetables.

Nutritional Information:
Calories: 549, Fats: 29 grams, Carbohydrates: 60.3 grams, Protein: 13.8 grams

Serves: 4 to 6
Cooking Time: 35 minutes

Ingredients:
- 1 tbsp. olive oil
- 4 cloves garlic, minced
- 3 strips lemon zest
- 1 jar chunky salsa
- 1 can tomato sauce
- 20 large shrimp, peeled and deveined
- 2 cups baby spinach
- ¼ cup crumbled feta cheese
- flatbread

Directions:

1. Heat olive oil in large cast-iron skillet, over medium-high heat. Add minced garlic and lemon zest and sauté until beginning to turn brown.

2. Add salsa and tomato sauce. Mix well and bring to a simmer. Add shrimp to tomato mixture, cover skillet and cook for 3 minutes or until shrimp turns pink.

3. Fold in spinach, stir and cook about 1 to 2 minutes or until spinach starts to wilt and shrimp is opaque.

4. Sprinkle feta cheese over top of shrimp and serve with flatbread or cooked orzo.

Nutritional Information:
Calories: 239, Fats: 6.8 grams, Carbohydrates: 35.7 grams, Protein: 11.8 grams

Serves: 4
Cooking Time: 15 minutes

Ingredients:
- 1 pound salmon fillet (skinned, cut into pieces)
- 1 tbsp. olive oil
- 1 tsp. curry powder
- 2 cloves garlic, minced
- 1 eggplant (cut into cubes)
- 14 oz. coconut milk (light)
- 2 tbsp. fish sauce
- 1 tbsp. brown sugar
- 2 cups sugar snap peas, trimmed
- ½ cup basil (chopped)

Directions:

1. Start by heating the oil in large cast-iron skillet over medium heat. Add the curry powder along with garlic and cook for approximately a minute or two

2. Next, add the cubed eggplant and cook an additional 2 minutes.

3. In small bowl, mix together the milk with sugar and fish sauce. Add the mixture to your skillet and bring it to boil.

4. Stir in the peas followed by salmon. Now cover and allow it to simmer for 5 minutes or until the salmon is well cooked.

5. Remove from heat and sprinkle the basil on top.

Nutritional Information:
Calories: 332 Fats: 15 grams, Carbohydrates: 21 grams, Protein: 28 grams

Serves: 4
Cooking Time: 35 minutes

Country Skillet Dinner

Ingredients:
- 1 pound ground beef
- 1 tbsp. vegetable oil
- ½ cup diced onion
- 2 cups hot water
- 1 (14 ounce) can tomato sauce
- 2 cups thin noodles, uncooked
- 1 small can mushrooms
- 1 tsp. oregano
- 1 cup mozzarella cheese, shredded

Directions:

1. Heat oil in large cast-iron skillet, over medium-high heat. Cook ground beef until brown, add onion and cook until translucent. Drain excess fat.

2. Turn heat to medium-low and layer uncooked noodles over ground beef mixture.

3. In medium bowl, mix together tomato sauce, mushrooms, and oregano. Pour over noodles, cover and simmer for 15 minutes, stirring frequently to avoid sticking.

4. Uncover and sprinkle cheese over top. Continue to simmer until cheese melts.

Nutritional Information:
Calories: 638 Fats: 12 grams, Carbohydrates: 43.2 grams, Protein: 22 grams

Serves: 5
Cooking Time: 20 minutes

Ingredients:

- 8 oz. flank steak, halved
- 1 tbsp. all-purpose flour
- 1 1/3 cups onion, sliced
- 1 green bell pepper, sliced
- 1 orange bell pepper, sliced
- 1 tsp. black pepper
- cooking spray
- 12 oz. pizza dough
- 1 tbsp. cornmeal
- 2 tsp. olive oil
- 5 garlic cloves, sliced
- 1 ½ tsp. soy sauce
- ½ cup low fat milk
- 2 ounces cheddar cheese, shredded
- ¼ tsp. onion powder
- 1/8 tsp. salt
- 1/8 tsp. ground red pepper

Directions:

1. Place a heavy baking sheet or pizza stone in cold oven. Leaving the baking sheet or stone in oven, preheat to 500 °F.

2. Spray a large cast-iron skillet with cooking spray and heat over medium-high. While skillet is heating, sprinkle steak with half of the black ground pepper. Add steak and cook for 4 minutes on each side or until meat reaches the desired doneness. Remove steak from skillet and let rest for 5 minutes. Cut into very thin slices, across the meat grain. Set aside.

3. Coat a medium size, microwave-safe bowl with cooking spray and add pizza dough. Cover with a towel or plastic wrap and microwave at 50% power

for 45 seconds. Remove from oven and let set for 5 minutes.

4. On floured surface, roll pizza dough into a 14-inch circle. With a fork, pierce dough, covering entire surface.

5. Remove hot pizza stone from oven and sprinkle with cornmeal. Carefully slide dough onto the pizza stone.

6. Bake until crust crisps and turns golden brown, about 10 minutes.

7. While crust is baking, place skillet over medium-high heat. Lightly coat bottom of skillet with olive oil. Add onions and green and orange bell peppers. Stirring constantly, sauté for 3 minutes. Add sliced garlic; sauté for 2 minutes and add steak and sauté for an additional 30 to 45 seconds. Remove from heat.

8. Remove pizza crust from oven. Add remaining ½ tsp. ground black pepper and soy sauce. Stir until mixed together and spread evenly over pizza crust.

9. In a microwave safe bowl, combine milk and flour and mix with a whisk until smooth. Microwave on HIGH for 2 minutes until thickened and stirring every 30 seconds. Add Cheese, onion powder, salt, and ground red pepper to hot milk mixture. Stir until cheese is melted and mixture is smooth.

10. Drizzle cheese sauce over pizza and cut in to 8 slices. Serve hot.

Nutritional Information:
Calories: 424, Fats: 10.3 grams, Carbohydrates: 53.6 grams, Protein: 25.9 grams

Serves: 4
Cooking Time: 30 minutes

Ingredients:

- 3 slices whole wheat country bread (5 to 6 ounces), crusts removed
- 2 tbsp. plus 1 tsp. extra virgin olive oil, divided
- ½ tsp. freshly ground black pepper, plus a pinch, divided
- 4 ounces lamb merguez sausage, or Italian chicken, turkey or pork sausage links
- 2 cloves garlic, thinly sliced
- 1 bunch broccoli rabe (about 12 ounces), trimmed and coarsely chopped
- 2 cups cooked cannellini beans, plus 1/2 cup bean cooking liquid or water
- ½ tsp. salt, plus a pinch, divided
- 4 large eggs

Directions:

1. Preheat oven to 400 °F.

2. Tear bread into irregular pieces, about ½ to 1 inch pieces. Drizzle 1 tbsp. of olive oil on large baking sheet, add bread and toss in oil. Sprinkle with ½ tsp. black pepper and bake for 10 to 12 minutes or until bread pieces are crisp and golden brown.

3. While bread pieces are baking, heat 1 tbsp. olive oil in a large cast-iron skillet over medium heat. Remove sausage casings and crumble while adding to the skillet. Cook for 3 to 5 minutes and sausage is brown. Remove sausage to a plate lined with paper towels and let skillet cool.

4. Remove leftover oil from skillet, place over medium heat and add remaining tbsp. of olive oil. Add garlic and sauté, stirring constantly for about 30 seconds or garlic becomes fragrant.

5. Add broccoli rabe to garlic and olive oil. Cook, stirring constantly, for 4 to 6 minutes until the rabe becomes tender and wilts but is still bright green. If greens start to dry out during cooking, add 1 to 2 tbsp. of water.

6. Add beans to the skillet along with the cooking liquid or water, sausage, and ½ tsp. salt. Stir to combine and bring mixture to a simmer.

7. Make 4 wells in the bean mixture and add an egg to each indention and season with remaining salt and pepper. Cover pan and cook eggs, checking frequently for desired firmness. For soft yolks, about 3 to 5 minutes, hard yolks, about 7 to 9 minutes.

8. Remove from heat and top with bread pieces. Serve while hot.

Nutritional Information:
Calories: 463, Fats: 24 grams, Carbohydrates: 25 grams, Protein: 9 grams

Serves: 4
Cooking Time: 45 minutes

Couscous Chicken

Ingredients:
- 12 oz. chicken, cooked and chopped
- 2 tbsp. olive oil
- 2 cups vegetable broth
- 2 cups onion, chopped
- 2 cups carrots, sliced thinly
- 2 cups celery, diced
- ½ tsp. salt
- ½ tsp. pepper
- 2 cloves garlic, minced
- 1⅓ cups pearl couscous

Directions:

1. Add the oil to a large, cast-iron skillet and heat over medium heat. Add the vegetables and sauté for approximately 10 minutes or until the vegetables turn soft and caramelized.

2. Stir in garlic and cook for a few minutes.

3. Next, stir in the vegetable broth and couscous.

4. Reduce the heat and cover the skillet, allowing it to simmer for 6 to 10 minutes.

5. Add chicken and cook about 2 minutes, stirring constantly, until chicken is heated through.

Nutritional Information:
Calories: 480, Fats: 10 grams, Carbohydrates: 57.9 grams, Protein: 36 grams

Serves: 4
Cooking Time: 20 minutes

Ingredients:
- 1 tbsp. olive oil
- 1 1 pound halibut filet, cut into 4 equal pieces
- 1 large yellow onion, thinly sliced
- 2 cloves garlic, minced
- 1 14 ½ ounce can diced tomatoes
- 1 9 ounce can cannellini beans, rinsed and drained
- 1 12 ounce jar roasted red peppers, drained and sliced
- 3 tbsp. chopped fresh sage or 1 tbsp. dried sage
- 1 tsp. kosher salt
- 1 tsp. freshly ground black pepper

Directions:

1. Place 12 inch cast-iron skillet over medium-high heat and add olive oil.

2. Sear halibut filets for 4 to 6 minutes or until golden brown on each side. Remove to plate and set aside.

3. Add sliced onions and minced garlic to skillet. Sauté 5 to 7 minutes or until softened.

4. Add tomatoes, beans, and red peppers to onion and garlic and stir until combined. Return halibut filets to skillet and simmer for 10 to 15 minutes or until fish is flakey and cooked through. Mix in sage, salt, and pepper.

5. Serve while hot.

Nutritional Information:
Calories: 270, Fats: 7 grams, Carbohydrates: 24 grams, Protein: 28 grams

Serves: 4
Cooking Time: 45 minutes

Roasted Chicken and Vegetables

Ingredients:

- 1 (4 to 5 pound) roasting chicken
- 1 tsp. curry powder
- 1 tsp. dried sage
- 1 tsp. dried rosemary
- 1 tsp. dried coriander
- 1 tsp. dried thyme
- 1 clove garlic, finely crushed
- 2 large carrots, cut into large chunks
- 2 large potatoes, cut into large chunks
- 1 parsnip, cut into large chunks
- ½ butternut squash, cut into large chunks
- 1 medium onion, cut into large chunks

Directions:

1. Preheat oven to 350 °F.

2. Place a round roasting rack in a large, deep cast-iron skillet (can also use a cast-iron Dutch oven).

3. Remove giblets from chicken cavity. Pat chicken dry, inside and out, with clean paper towels, changing as needed. Place chicken on roasting rack, breast side down, and tuck legs underneath chicken.

4. In small bowl, add curry powder, sage, rosemary, coriander, and thyme. Whisk together until well blended. Separate out 2 tsp. of rub and ¼ cup of olive oil, blend well and set aside.

5. Vigorously rub remaining chicken rub over the outside of the chicken, making sure to cover all creases and folds.

6. Arrange chopped vegetables and crushed garlic around chicken.

7. Cover skillet and place on middle rack of preheated oven. Cook for approximately 1 hour, liberally basting chicken and vegetables with the chicken rub and olive oil mixture, about every 15 to 20 minutes.

8. Uncover skillet after 1 hour and bake an additional 15 to 30 minutes or until chicken skin is brown and an inserted meat thermometer reads an internal temperature of 165 °F and juices run clear when cut at the thickest part of the chicken.

9. Remove from pan and let chicken rest for 10 minutes before carving.

Nutritional Information:
Calories: 386, Fats: 12 grams, Carbohydrates: 32 grams, Protein: 16 grams

Serves: 4
Cooking Time: 90 minutes

Ingredients:

- 1 pound rigatoni noodles
- 8 ounces ricotta cheese
- 4 ounces goat cheese
- 1 tsp. kosher salt
- 1 tsp. ground black pepper
- 3 cups marinara sauce
- 6 or 7 fresh basil leaves, finely chopped
- ½ cup finely grated parmesan cheese

Directions:

1. Preheat oven to 350 °F.

2. Bring a large pot of salted water to a boil. Add rigatoni and cook al dente, according to package directions. Drain, rinse with cool water, and set aside.

3. In a medium bowl, add ricotta and goat cheese and mix well. Stir in kosher salt and ground black pepper.

4. Fill a pastry bag or a Ziploc bag, with the end snipped off, with cheese mixture. Pipe cheese mixture into cooked rigatoni noodles.

5. Pour 1 cup of marinara sauce into a 10 inch, cast-iron skillet and spread over bottom. Sprinkle sauce with chopped basil leaves.

6. Place noodles in a circle around the skillet, one layer at a time.

7. Pour remaining 2 cups of marinara sauce over top of stuffed rigatoni noodles. Sprinkle the top of sauce with grated parmesan cheese.

8. Place skillet on middle rack of preheated oven and bake for 15 minutes or until the noodle edges start turning golden brown and sauce is bubbly.

Nutritional Information:
Calories: 247, Fats: 18 grams, Carbohydrates: 41 grams, Protein: 11 grams

Serves: 6
Cooking Time: 25 minutes

Ingredients:

- 1 cup masa harina
- 1 tsp. kosher salt, divided
- ¼ tsp. ground red pepper
- 1 cup boiling water
- 1 tbsp. olive oil
- 8 ounces ground sirloin
- 1 ½ cups chopped onion
- 3 garlic cloves, minced
- 1 poblano chili pepper, seeded and chopped
- ½ tsp. freshly ground black pepper
- 1 cup frozen baby lima beans
- 8 ounces tomatillos (about 8 small), chopped
- 2 tbsp. butter, melted
- ½ tsp. baking powder
- ¼ cup (1 ounce) crumbled queso fresco
- 2 tbsp. chopped fresh cilantro
- 4 lime wedges, optional

Directions:

1. Preheat oven to 400 °F.

2. In medium bowl, add masa harina, ½ tsp. kosher salt and ground red pepper. Mix with a wire whisk until ingredients are well blended.

3. Add boiling water to the whisked masa mixture and stir with a spoon until ingredients form a soft dough. Cover and set aside.

4. Place a 9 inch cast-iron skillet over medium-high heat, and add enough olive oil to coat the bottom of the skillet. Add ground sirloin and cook until brown and crumbly, about 5 minutes.

5. To ground meat, add onion, minced garlic, poblano chili pepper, remaining kosher salt, and ground

black pepper and mix well. Stirring frequently, sauté until onions are translucent.

6. Add lima beans and chopped tomatillos to the meat mixture. Stir and cook for 2 minutes. Remove from heat and set aside.

7. Remove cover from masa dough and add baking powder and melted butter. Stir until dough is smooth.

8. With a spoon, place dollops of masa dough over meat filling and spread into an even layer with the back of spoon, making sure to take dough to the edges of the skillet.

9. Cover skillet with aluminum foil and place on center rack of preheated oven. Bake for 30 minutes. Remove foil and bake an additional 10 minutes or until the crust turns a golden brown around the edges.

10. Remove from oven and let rest for 3 minutes, then sprinkle top of skillet pie with queso fresco and chopped cilantro. If desired, serve with lime wedges.

Nutritional Information:
Calories: 378, Fats: 15.2 grams, Carbohydrates: 43.4 grams, Protein: 20.5 grams

Serves: 4
Cooking Time: 1 hour, 10 minutes

Ingredients:
- 1 tbsp. extra virgin olive oil
- 12 ounces chicken sausage (cooked and sliced)
- 1 medium onion, thinly sliced
- 3 medium potatoes, sliced
- 1 ½ cups sauerkraut, rinsed
- 1 ½ cups dry white wine
- ½ tsp. freshly ground pepper
- ¼ tsp. caraway seeds
- 1 bay leaf

Directions:

1. Add oil to large cast-iron skillet and heat over medium heat. Add cooked chicken sausage and sliced onion. Cook meat and onions, stirring frequently, about 4 minutes or until meat starts turning brown.

2. Add sliced potatoes, sauerkraut, and wine. Mix well, then add black pepper, caraway seeds, and bay leaf. Stir mixture and bring to a simmer, cover and cook for 10 to 15 minutes or until most of the liquid has cooked away and potatoes are tender. Stir frequently to keep from sticking to the bottom of the skillet.

3. Remove bay leaf before serving.

Nutritional Information:
Calories: 295, Fats: 9 grams, Carbohydrates: 24 grams, Protein: 14 grams

Serves: 4
Cooking Time: 30 minutes

Ingredients:
Chicken Pie Filling

- 1/3 cup butter
- 1/3 cup all-purpose flour
- 1 ½ cups chicken broth
- 1½ cups milk
- 1 ½ tsp. creole seasoning
- 2 tbsp. butter
- 1 onion, diced
- 8 oz. mushrooms, sliced
- 4 cups cooked chicken, chopped
- 2 cups hash browns, frozen, cubed
- 1 cup matchstick carrots
- 1 cup green sweet peas, frozen
- 1/3 cup parsley, chopped

Pastry Crust

- 1 14.1 oz. package piecrust
- 1 egg, beaten

Directions:

1. Preheat oven to 350 °F.

2. In a large saucepan, over medium heat, melt butter. Stirring constantly with a wire whisk, add flour and mix until sauce is smooth and starts to bubble and thicken, about 1 minute.

3. Slowly add chicken broth and milk, continuing a constant whisking. Cook for 6 to 7 minutes or until gravy starts to thicken and bubble. Stir in creole seasoning and remove from heat.

4. Place large Dutch oven over medium-high heat and melt butter. Add mushrooms and onions and sauté until tender, about 10 minutes.

5. Add chopped chicken, hash browns, carrots, green sweet peas, and fresh parsley to mushrooms and onions and stir until mixed. Add gravy and mix well, cooking until mixture just starts to simmer. Remove from heat.

6. Place 1 ready-made pie crust in a 10 inch, lightly greased cast-iron skillet. Gently stretch crust, without tearing, to fit the skillet, if needed.

7. Pour chicken mixture over pie crust. Using a spoon, spread mixture evenly over the crust.

8. Top pot pie with remaining pie crust, stretching if necessary. Pinch edges of crust to the rim of the cast-iron skillet.

9. Brush pie crust top with beaten egg. Make 4 or 5 slits in top crust to help steam escape.

10. Place skillet on center rack of preheated oven. Bake for 1 hour or until crust is golden brown and chicken mixture is bubbly.

Nutritional Information:
Calories: 495, Fats: 25.0 grams, Carbohydrates: 45 grams, Protein: 22 grams

Serves: 6 to 8
Cooking Time: 1 hour

Seafood Paella

Ingredients:
- 4 cups clam juice
- ¼ cup extra virgin olive oil
- 1 onion, chopped
- 1 small green bell pepper, coarsely chopped
- 3 large cloves garlic, finely chopped
- salt and pepper
- 2 tbsp. tomato paste
- 1 tsp. paprika
- ½ tsp. crumbled saffron
- 1½ cups short grain rice
- 1 cup dry white wine
- 1 pound small clams, scrubbed
- ½ pound large shrimp

Directions:

1. Preheat the oven to 425 °F. In a saucepan, bring the clam juice to a simmer over medium heat.

2. Preheat a large (10 to 12 inch) cast-iron skillet over medium-high heat. Add the extra virgin olive oil, onion, bell pepper, garlic, 1 tsp. salt and ¾ tsp. pepper and cook, stirring occasionally, until the onion is golden, about 5 minutes. Add the tomato paste, paprika, and saffron and cook, stirring, for 1 minute.

3. Add the rice, stirring to coat, then stir in the wine. Bring to a boil, cooking until the liquid is reduced by half, about 2 minutes. Add the hot clam juice, stir once, then bring to a boil and cook for 5 minutes.

4. Add the clams, then transfer the paella to the oven. Bake until the clams open, about 30 minutes. Nestle the shrimp into the paella. Bake until the rice is cooked through and the shrimps are opaque, about 5 minutes. Let cool for 5 minutes before serving.

Nutritional Information:
Calories: 256, Fats: 11 grams, Carbohydrates: 32 grams, Protein: 16 grams

Serves: 4
Cooking Time: 1 hour

Ingredients:
- ½ cup of water
- 4 chicken breasts, boneless and skinless
- 1 tbsp. extra virgin olive oil
- 3 tbsp. of maple syrup
- 1/3 cup of apple cider vinegar
- 1 tbsp. of fresh thyme
- 1 tsp. of salt
- ½ cup of chopped walnuts
- ¼ tsp of pepper

Directions:

1. Mix the pepper, salt, olive oil, and the thyme together
2. Rub the chicken with the seasoning and set aside for now
3. Preheat a large (10 to 12 inch) cast-iron skillet over medium-high heat. Add the extra virgin olive oil and toast the walnuts for about six minutes
4. Move the walnuts to the dish and put the heat on high for the skillet
5. Put the chicken in the cast-iron skillet and let it cook for 12 minutes, turn every couple of minutes
6. Put the chicken on the clean plate
7. Add the vinegar to the chicken and let it cook for another minute, stir constantly
8. Add in the maple syrup and the water, let it cook for another seven minutes
9. Stir in the walnuts
10. Remove from heat
11. Serve and enjoy

Nutritional Facts:
Calories: 292; Fat: 14.3g; Carbohydrates: 12.3g;
Protein: 29.8g

Serves: 2
Cooking Time: 30 minutes

Ingredients:
- 3 tbsp. of fresh parsley, chopped
- 1 pound of boneless leg of lamb, cut into 1 inch pieces
- 4 large red bell peppers, sliced into rings
- 2 cups of hot water
- ¼ tsp. of salt
- ½ tsp. of pepper
- 2 garlic cloves, minced
- 3 tbsp. of coconut oil

Directions:

1. Cover both sides of the lamb with the salt and the pepper and set aside

2. Heat up the coconut oil in a large cast-iron skillet on medium high

3. Place the lamb pieces in it and cook for approximately 5 minutes. Be sure to brown the lamb on all sides.

4. Add the water and the garlic to the pan and let it come to a boil

5. After it is boiling, reduce the heat to medium and cook for 30 to 40 minutes or until the lamb is tender

6. Mix in the red pepper and let it cook for another 10 minutes

7. Remove from heat and put it on a plate

8. Top with the fresh parsley

Nutritional Facts:
Calories: 354; Fat: 19.0g; Carbohydrates: 10.7g; Protein: 33.7g

Serves 4

Cooking Time: 55 minutes

Pear Curry

Ingredients:
- 3 boneless chicken breasts, halved, cut into cubes
- 1 pear, peeled, cored and pureed
- 1 pear, cored, cubed
- 14 ounces light coconut milk
- 1 cup onion, diced
- ¾ tsp. ground ginger
- 1 tsp. minced garlic
- ¾ tsp. ground cinnamon
- 1 tbsp. curry powder
- 1 tbsp. vegetable oil
- ¼ tsp. ground black pepper
- ⅓ cup raisins, optional

Directions:

1. In a large cast-iron skillet, heat the vegetable oil over medium heat. Add the diced onions, curry powder, cinnamon, ginger, garlic, salt and pepper and sauté for approximately 5 to 7 minutes.
2. Add the chicken breasts and continue to sauté for an additional 5 to 10 minutes or until the chicken turns brown.
3. Pour in the pear puree, milk and raisins. Allow it to simmer for 3 to 5 minutes.
4. Next, add the pear cubes on top and continue to simmer for an additional five minutes.

Nutritional Facts:
Calories: 383; Fat 10g; Carbohydrates 24g; Protein 3.5g

Serves 6
Cooking Time: 55 minutes

Ingredients

- 1 lb. chicken breast, chunks
- 1 tbsp. sesame oil
- 1 large onion, diced
- 4 large lettuce leaves
- 1 tomato, diced
- 1 avocado, pitted and cut in chunks
- 1 tbsp. lime juice
- 2 tbsp. garlic, minced
- a few fresh cilantro leaves, washed and finely chopped
- 1 jalapeño, chopped

Directions:

1. Preheat a large (10 to 12 inch) cast-iron skillet over medium-high heat. Add the extra virgin olive oil to it.

2. Next, add the chicken along with garlic and sprinkle the lime juice until the pieces are nicely brown and cooked thoroughly.

3. When the chicken is cooked, add the vegetables and spices (all but the avocado) and cook together for just a few moments.

4. Remove from heat and place a scoop of the chicken mixture into a large lettuce leaf.

5. Top it off with a few chunks of avocado and a dash of salt and pepper.

Nutritional Information:
Calories: 322, Fats: 11 grams, Carbohydrates: 28 grams, Protein: 8 grams

Serves: 4
Cooking Time: 35 minutes

Ingredients
- 1 lb. flank steak, thinly sliced
- 2 tbsp. sesame oil, for cooking
- 3 cloves of garlic, minced
- 2 tsp. fresh ginger, grated
- ½ cup soy sauce
- 3 tbsp. honey
- 1 tsp. sesame oil
- 1 red bell pepper, thinly sliced
- 1 orange bell pepper, thinly sliced
- 1 red onion, thinly sliced
- 1 cup mushrooms, sliced
- 1 handful green onions, chopped

Directions

1. Preheat a large (10 to 12 inch) cast-iron skillet over medium-high heat.

2. Add the sesame oil to it and sauté ginger and garlic. Turn heat on low and add the soy sauce.

3. Turn the heat up to a medium low and add honey, sesame oil, and fish sauce.

4. Bring the sauce to a boil slowly, add in mushrooms, onions, and peppers, and cook until the onion is soft, around 7 minutes. Remove vegetables with slotted spoon.

5. Increase heat of the cast-iron skillet to medium high and add the steak. Cook the steak on each side for 2 to 3 minutes until cooked through.

6. Add the vegetables back to the pan and mix well. Top with green onions.

7. Serve hot

Nutritional Information:

Calories: 521, Fats: 22 grams, Carbohydrates: 36.8 grams, Protein: 16 grams

Serves: 3
Cooking Time: 30 minutes

Ingredients:
- 2 cup tomatoes
- 1 can white beans
- 2 tbsp. capers
- 1 tbsp. minced garlic
- 2 tbsp. olive oil
- ¼ tsp. salt
- 1 pound shrimp
- ¾ cup stock

Directions:

1. Toss capers, tomatoes, garlic, beans, oil, and salt in a bowl.
2. In another bowl, toss shrimp with a bit of oil and a quarter tsp. of salt.
3. Preheat cast-iron skillet in oven for 15 minutes.
4. Remove it from oven and toss the tomato mixture and broil.
5. Now, remove from oven and add the stock with shrimp.
6. Broil and stir for 3 minutes until the shrimps are opaque.
7. Drizzle with oil and serve with rice.

Nutritional Information:
Calories: 248, Fats: 8 grams, Carbohydrates: 23 grams, Protein: 11 grams

Serves: 4
Cooking Time: 20 minutes

Ingredients:
- ½ cup porcini mushrooms, dried
- 1 cup water, boiling
- 3 cups button mushrooms, chopped
- 2 tbsp. oil
- 1/8 tsp. black pepper
- 2 garlic cloves
- 1 cup finely chopped onions
- 2 1/4 cup water
- 1 cup barley, uncooked
- ½ tsp. salt
- ¼ cup parsley, fresh
- 1 tbsp. butter

Directions:

1. Add the dried porcini mushrooms in boiling water and cover it for 15 minutes.
2. Strain and reserve the stock and chop them.
3. In a cast-iron skillet, heat oil and ¾ of the amount chopped button mushrooms and sauté. Add porcini mushrooms, pepper and garlic and cook till water is reduced.
4. In sauce pan, add oil and cook onions till soft.
5. Add the reserved mushroom mixture and add porcini mixture, water, barley and salt and bring to boil.
6. Let it simmer on low heat for 35 minutes till barley is tender.
7. Stir with fork and add parsley.
8. Sauté the leftover mushrooms in butter and garnish on the pilaf.

Nutritional Information:
Calories: 322, Fats: 10 grams, Carbohydrates: 28 grams, Protein: 9 grams

Serves: 4
Cooking time: 50 minutes

Ingredients:
Chermoula

- 1 cup fresh chopped parsley
- 1 tbsp. paprika
- 3 tbsp. broth
- 2 tbsp. lime juice
- 1 tbsp. olive oil
- 1 tsp. cumin
- ¼ tsp. salt
- ½ tsp. ground coriander
- ¼ tsp. red pepper
- 2 garlic cloves

Steak

- 1 1.5 lb. steak, meat to be as per your wish
- ¼ tsp. salt
- ¼ tsp. black pepper

Directions:

1. Blend all the ingredients for sauce in food processor to form a thick creamy texture.
2. Sprinkle salt and pepper on the steak and grill it in the oil sprayed cast-iron grill pan.
3. Cook for approximately 4 to 5 minutes or until well done.
   Allow it to rest for 5 minutes; cut it into slices and serve with sauce.

Nutritional Information:
Calories: 195, Fats: 9 grams, Carbohydrates: 24 grams, Protein: 11 grams

Serves: 6
Cooking Time: 45 minutes

Spiced Sirloin Steak

Ingredients:
- 1 tbsp. brown sugar
- ½ tsp. salt
- ½ tsp. cumin, ground
- ½ tsp. coriander seeds, ground
- 1 pound boneless sirloin steak
- ¼ tsp. ground red peppers

Directions:

1. Preheat the oven to 450 °F.
2. Spray the oil in an 8 inch cast-iron skillet and place in the preheated oven
3. Mix brown sugar, salt, cumin, coriander and pepper and marinate the steak in the spice mixture.
4. Place the steak in the preheated pan and allow it to bake for approximately 7 to10 minutes or until well done.
5. Let it rest and cut it in thin slices.
6. Serve with desired vegetables.

Nutritional Information:
Calories: 201, Fats: 8.6 grams, Carbohydrates: 23 grams, Protein: 13 grams

Serves: 4
Cooking Time: 20 minutes

Ingredients:
- 2 trout fillets
- 4 sprigs thyme
- 4 tbsp. butter
- 1 lemon, sliced
- 1 lemon, juiced
- 1 tbsp. parsley
- salt and pepper to taste

Directions:

1. Melt the butter in a cast-iron skillet.

2. In the meantime, place the trout in a shallow dish and season it with salt and pepper.

3. Place the trout in the buttered skillet skinned down along with thyme and lemon.

4. Cook for approximately 5 to 7 minutes and transfer to the plate.

5. Pour the sauce over fish and serve!

Nutritional Information:
Calories: 198, Fats: 6.9 grams, Carbohydrates: 32 grams, Protein: 16 grams

Serves: 2
Cooking Time: 10 minutes

Ingredients:
- 1 lb. gnocchi
- kosher salt to taste
- ground black pepper to taste
- 9 oz. chicken sausage, cooked and sliced
- 1 pint cherry tomatoes, sliced
- 1 oz. basil, fresh

Directions:

1. Boil a pot of salted water and cook gnocchi for approximately 2 minutes, drizzle with olive oil.
2. Heat a cast-iron skillet with a little oil and add the sausage to it.
3. Cook for approximately 10 to 12 minutes or until it browns. Push sausage to the edge and keep warm.
4. Stir in the tomatoes followed by the gnocchi. Cook for another 7 to 8 minutes.
5. Add in the basil and sprinkle the salt and pepper on top.
6. Serve immediately

Nutritional Information:
Calories: 295, Fats: 15.0 grams, Carbohydrates: 32 grams, Protein: 12 grams

Serves: 4
Cooking time: 20 minutes

Ingredients:
- 1 beef tenderloin steak
- 1/2 medium onion, thick sliced
- 1/2 pound tomatoes, plum
- 2 tbsp. oil
- 1 tbsp. lemon juice
- 1 tsp. brown sugar
- 1.5 tsp. chipotle chili powder
- 2 large garlic cloves, minced
- 5/8 tsp. salt
- 1/4 tsp. oregano
- 1/4 tsp. black pepper
- 1 red bell pepper, halved
- 8 corn tortillas
- 1/4 cup sour cream

Directions:

1. In a small mixing bowl, combine the oil with lemon juice, brown sugar, chili powder, and a garlic clove and mix well.

2. Place the steak in a shallow dish and pour the marinade on top. Coat the steak evenly with the marinade.

3. Cover and allow it to sit for approximately 20 to 30 minutes.

4. Brush a grill pan with some oil. Add onion slices, tomatoes and bell pepper to it. Season it with oregano and pepper and cook for 4 minutes or until the veggies become charred.

5. Puree the tomatoes with a quarter tsp. of salt and a garlic clove in food processor, set aside.

6. In large cast-iron skillet, covered with oil, add the steak along with the mixture and cook till desired doneness.

7. Heat the tortillas and serve with steak, veggies and sour cream.

Nutritional Information:
Calories 336, Fat 17g, Protein 22g, carbohydrate 26 g

Serves: 4
Cooking Time: 45 minutes

Tarragon Chicken

Ingredients:
- 1 lemon juice
- 1/3 heavy cream
- 1/2 tsp. salt
- 1/2 cup flour
- 1 tbsp. butter
- 3 large chicken breast, boneless
- 1/4 tsp. white pepper
- 1 tsp. oil
- 1 cup broth
- 1/2 cup peas
- 3 tbsp. minced tarragon

Directions:

1. In bowl, mix together the lemon juice with cream and salt, set aside.

2. In other bowl, mash 1 tsp. flour with 1 tsp. butter to form paste.

3. Season chicken with remaining salt and pepper and dredge slightly in flour, shake off the excess.

4. Heat the butter in a large cast-iron skillet and add the chicken to it. Allow it to cook until the chicken turns brown.

5. Add 1/2 cup broth to it and allow it to simmer for 4 to 6 minutes.

6. Transfer the chicken to a plate and cut into pieces.

7. Add the remaining broth to the pan and boil for 2 to 4 minutes.

8. Next, add lemon and cream to it and allow it simmer.

9. Whisk in butter and flour paste, a few bits at a time and add in the peas.

10. Reduce the heat and add chicken and tarragon and cook for 2 minutes.

11. Serve chicken with sauce and rice.

Nutritional Information:
Calories 231, Fat 10 g, Carbohydrates 91 g, Protein 28 g

Serves: 6
Cooking Time: 50 minutes

Sesame Chicken

Ingredients:
- 2 pounds boneless chicken, cubed
- ½ tsp. salt
- ½ tsp. pepper
- 3 tbsp. flour
- 2 tbsp. sesame oil
- 1 tbsp. olive oil
- 2 garlic cloves
- 1 tbsp. soy sauce
- 1 tbsp. brown sugar
- 1 tbsp. vinegar
- ½ cup chicken stock
- 3 tbsp. sesame seeds

Directions:

1. In a bowl, whisk together the chicken stock with sugar, 1 tbsp. sesame oil, garlic, soy sauce, and vinegar.
2. Preheat the oven to 400 °F.
3. Heat the oil in a large cast-iron skillet.
4. Toss in the chicken and season it with salt, pepper and flour. Allow it to cook until the chicken turns brown.
5. Pour the chicken stock mixture and toss.
6. Bake in the oven for 20 minutes.
7. Remove and cover with sesame seeds.
8. Serve with veggies

Nutritional Information:
Calories: 332 Fats: 14 grams, Carbohydrates: 26 grams, Protein: 13 grams

Serves: 3
Cooking Time: 35 minutes

Turkey Chili

Ingredients:
- 1 ounce of sausage
- 1 tbsp. oil
- 2 turkey cutlets, pieces
- 1 tbsp. cumin
- 1.5 tsp. garlic powder
- salt and pepper to taste
- 2 chopped onions
- 4 cans kidney beans
- 2 whole jalapeno peppers
- 3 cans chicken broth

Directions:

1. Preheat the oven to 350 °F.
2. Bake the sausages for 30 minutes and chop.
3. Heat the olive oil in a large cast-iron skillet. Add turkey to it and cook for approximately 5 minutes.
4. Add cumin, garlic powder, salt and pepper and mix.
5. Add the onions and cook for an additional 5 minutes or until the onions turn soft.
6. Add kidney beans and broth and allow it to simmer for 30 minutes.
7. Mix the chopped jalapenos and sausage and stir.
8. Cook for 15 minutes or until the chili turns tender.
9. Serve with rice

Nutritional Information:
Calories: 537, Fats: 23.0 grams, Carbohydrates: 53 grams, Protein: 19 grams

Serves: 6
Cooking time: 45 minutes

Ingredients:

- 2 lb. chicken breasts, boneless
- ¼ cup almond flour
- ¼ cup arrowroot powder
- ¾ cup chicken broth
- 1 small onion, chopped
- 2 to 3 cloves of garlic, chopped
- 8 to 9 tbsp. grass-fed ghee
- ½ cup lemon juice, freshly squeezed
- ½ cup capers
- ¼ tsp. sea salt
- ¼ tsp. pepper
- ½ cup freshly chopped parsley, optional

Directions:

1. Start by cutting the chicken horizontally in halves so that you have 2 thin slices. Season it with sea salt and pepper.

2. In a mixing bowl, mix the flour and arrowroot powder. Dredge the chicken in the mixture and set aside.

3. In a large cast-iron skillet, heat approximately 4 tbsp. of bacon fat. Add garlic and onion to it.

4. Stir for 2 to 3 minutes and then add half of the chicken. Cook for 4 to 5 minutes on each side or until golden brown.

5. Set aside the first piece and cook the other piece of chicken in the remaining bacon fat.

6. Remove the chicken and place it on the cooling rack.

7. Next, add the chicken broth, lemon juice, capers and parsley, allowing it to cook for 3 to 4 minutes.

8. Add the chicken and cook for another 3 to 4 minutes.

9. Cover and allow it to simmer for 5 minutes.

10. Place the chicken on the serving platter and pour the remaining sauce over it.

11. Garnish and serve.

Nutritional Information:
Calories 679;   Fat 32.7g;   Carbohydrates 5.1g;
Protein 85.8g

Serves: 4
Cooking Time: 20 minutes

Conclusion

Cooking cast-iron dinner meals is the perfect choice for anyone who is looking to lose weight, remain active, lower their high blood pressure or even reduce their risk of developing heart problems. It also helps you out by limiting the amount of carbohydrates and fats that you are taking in each day so that you are effectively able to see the numbers on your scale go down with hardly any work.

CPSIA information can be obtained
at www.ICGtesting.com
Printed in the USA
LVOW04s2205061215
465693LV00024B/906/P